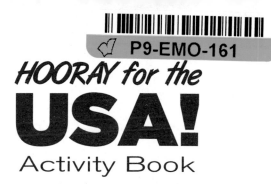

HOORAY for the
USA!
Activity Book

Becky J. Radtke

DOVER PUBLICATIONS, INC.
Mineola, New York

Bibliographical Note

Hooray for the USA! Activity Book is a new work,
first published by Dover Publications, Inc., in 2016.

International Standard Book Number

ISBN-13: 978-0-486-80780-5
ISBN-10: 0-486-80780-0

Manufactured in the United States by RR Donnelley
80780001   2016
www.doverpublications.com

This little activity book about the United States of America is full of fun and facts—there are crosswords, mazes, word puzzles, matching, and so much more. You'll be amazed at how many new things you will learn about the people and places that are part of U.S. history!

Do your best to solve the puzzles, but if you need a little help or want to check your answers, the Solutions start on page 43. Once you're finished with the puzzles, you can have even more fun coloring in the pictures with colored pencils, crayons, or markers.

free home brave
~~stripes~~ stars flag

The words above are all from America's National Anthem. Fit them into the crossword. One has already been written in to give you a start.

1

The U.S.A. is a democracy. Write the
above words in correct number order
to see what this means.

– – – –

– – – – – – – –

Spell the name of a well-known swampy area in Florida. Cross out the first lily pad and every other one after that. Then write the letters that remain in the blanks.

Did you know wild horses still can be
found in the Nevada desert? Circle the
two here that are exactly the same.

$\overline{}$ u f e e z

$\overline{}$ c f b s

Draw one in this space.

What popular toy was named after U.S. president Theodore Roosevelt? Write the letter that comes just before the one shown to spell out the answer.

Draw lines to match the shadows to
the presidents' faces that are carved
into Mount Rushmore above.

The Statue of Liberty was a gift from France.
It stands 305 feet tall. See how quickly
you can race up to the top of the torch!

Lake Michigan is the only Great Lake that is completely within the U.S. borders! Find the hidden letters that spell MICHIGAN and color them blue.

Each week country music fans flock to see this popular American show in Nashville, Tennessee. Find and color the hidden letters that spell GRAND OLE OPRY.

9

(And Sometimes)

ΛΕΙΟΥ ^ Y

H_RV_RD

_N_V_RS_T_

Pick from the list of vowels to finish spelling
the name of the oldest institution of higher
education in the United States,
established in 1636.

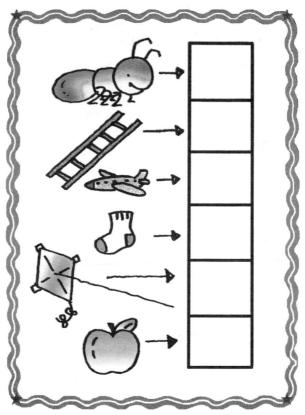

What is the largest U.S. state by size in square miles? Spell out the answer by writing the first letter of each picture in the box next to it.

The first S'mores recipe appeared in a 1927 Girl Scout handbook. Count how many times the word "S'more" appears in the picture and write that number in the blank.

Use the shape code to find the name of
a U.S. region that is mostly flat and
has great soil for growing crops.

As a first lady, Eleanor Roosevelt worked for social, racial, and political justice. Circle the two pictures of her above that are exactly the same.

Use the stars and stripes code to spell
out a name that our flag is often called.

President William McKinley used to whistle
the start of "Yankee Doodle." His musical
pet parrot would then complete it!

The song continues but six things have
changed here. As you spot each one,
draw a circle around it.

Yellowstone was the first National Park
created by Congress in 1872. It's a great
place to vacation in Wyoming and is
home to many types of wildlife.

Write the names of these animals that live in Yellowstone into the crossword. Some letters have been added to give you a bit of help.

Help this climber achieve her dream of reaching the top of Denali, formerly Mount McKinley, in Alaska. At 20,310 feet, it's the highest mountain in the U.S.A.

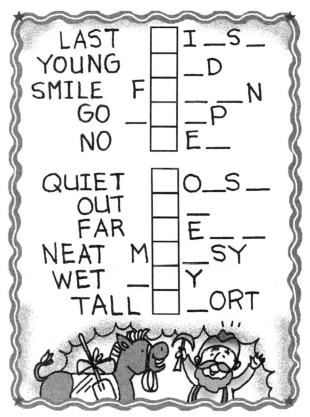

LAST	F	I_S_
YOUNG	O	_D
SMILE	F R	_ _N
GO	T	_P
NO	Y	E_

QUIET	N	O_S_
OUT	I	_
FAR	N	E_ _
NEAT	M E	_SY
WET	_ R	Y
TALL	S	_ORT

Write the opposite of each word given. The letters in the boxes will spell, from top to bottom, the nickname given to 1849 California gold seekers.

Fly... 4 left, 3 up, 6 right, 3 up, 1 left, 1 down, 2 left, and 1 up

Welcome!

Start

Sally Ride was the first American woman to travel into space. Follow the instructions at the top to help her take off!

GRAND CANYON

_____   _____

_____   _____

_____   _____

_____   _____

_____   _____

Try to fill all the lines with new words using
only the letters found in "Grand Canyon."
Around five million people visit it each year!

(Indiana)

_____

(North Carolina)

_____

(Tennessee)

_____

Use the picture and letter clues to sound
out the names of three state flowers.
Write them into the blanks.

1 2 3

	1	2	3
⇨	s	c	r
➡	a	m	t
◀	y	u	b

⇨2 ➡1 ⇨2 ➡3 ◀2 ⇨1

There's one now!

Use the grid to spell out the name of a plant found primarily in very dry areas of the southwestern United States.

"ASK NOT WHAT YOUR COUNTRY CAN DO FOR YOU; ASK WHAT YOU CAN DO FOR YOUR COUNTRY."

```
A S K D Y O U F
W O S L Q C K O
H U T W Y A S R
A P Y V O N L P
T T S K U L R V
D R H C R W A Q
O C O U N T R Y
```

Find and circle the underlined words in the famous statement, above, made by President John F. Kennedy. Look across and down in the puzzle.

The Fourth of July is when we celebrate America's birthday! Circle the three holiday food items that Sam can buy that will cost him <u>exactly</u> $1.50.

California is home to the tallest tree on Earth! Cross out the first leaf and every other one after that to find out the kind of tree it is.

It's believed the figure Uncle Sam is based on a New York meat packer, Sam Wilson. He sent beef to the troops during the War of 1812. Finish Sam's other half.

CO __ T

HEAR __

__ IPS

__ RM

SPOO __

CA __

B __ RD

__ AR

Finish spelling these words. Then read
the letters in the squares, from top to
bottom, to see which ocean is on the
east coast of America.

30

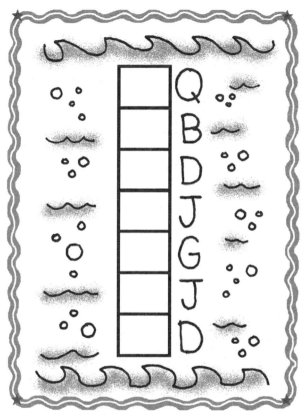

Write the letter that comes just before the one shown. When you're done, the letters listed from top to bottom will spell the name of the ocean on America's west coast.

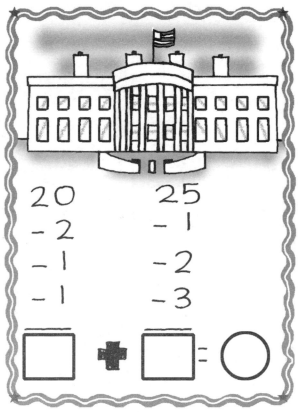

```
  20        25
  -2        -1
  -1        -2
  -1        -3
```

☐ ✚ ☐ = ◯

Besides the president, lots of people live in the White House! Solve the subtraction problems, then add their answers together to find out how many bathrooms it has.

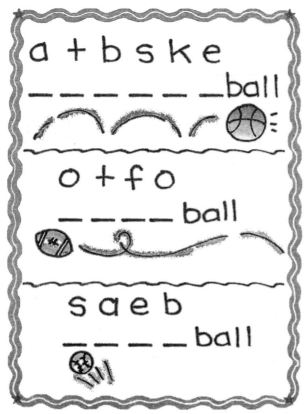

a + b s k e

_ _ _ _ _ _ _ _ ball

o + f o

_ _ _ _ _ ball

s a e b

_ _ _ _ _ ball

These three beloved American sports end
with the same word. Unscramble the letters
and write them into the blanks to finish
spelling each word.

33

Wisconsin dairy cows help produce our nation's supply of butter, cream, cheese, and (of course) milk!

Even though this scene might look like the
one opposite, seven things have changed.
Look closely and when you find them,
circle them.

Every state in America has its own flag.
Design one of your own for your state.
Make sure it shows some of the things
you love about the place you live!

Circle all of the uppercase letters in this puzzle. Then write them, in order, in the blanks to find a famous American invention that's in most households today.

Hawaii became our 50th state in 1959. Use the clues below to decide which lucky kid gets to call this beautiful place home! Circle him or her.

Clues: The child is wearing...
1. A sleeveless shirt. 2. A flower necklace.
3. Sunglasses. 4. A cap.

Help this hungry tourist find his way to a real town found in America. It sounds like it can offer some delicious breakfast food!

Write the first letter of each picture to
spell the name of an actual town in Oregon.

E T N S P U A

_ _ _ _ _ _ _

Unscramble these letters to spell what
Georgia grows more of than any other
U.S. state! You've probably eaten them as
a snack or part of a delicious spread!

```
O N T A R I O V B B
E S U P E R I O R T
H C Q J I O Z Q M Q
Q T Z H A H B H I V
V G N U A N E N C S
O Q S R M E Y K H X
F N H O R O X Z I M
Z T P N L S Z O G T
E R I E P E S Q A S
D E S S W F W Q N O
```

MICHIGAN
ERIE HURON
SUPERIOR
ONTARIO

Find and circle the names of the five
Great Lakes hidden in the puzzle. Look
across and down.

SOLUTIONS

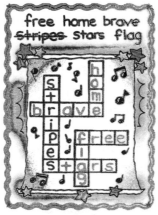

page 1

page 2

43

page 3

page 4

page 5

page 6

page 7

page 8

page 9

page 10

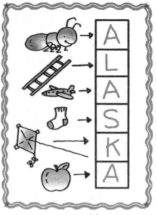

page 11

page 12

page 13

page 14

≈ = Y ☆ = O
★ = D ★★ = G
▬ = R ▭ = L

O L D
☆ ▭ ★

G L O R Y
★★ ▭ ☆ ▬ ≈

page 15

page 17

page 18

page 20

51

LAST   **F**IRST
YOUNG   **O**LD
SMILE   FR**O**WN
GO   S**T**OP
NO   **Y**ES

QUIET   **N**OISY
OUT   **I**N
FAR   **N**EAR
NEAT   ME**S**SY
WET   D**R**Y
TALL   **S**HORT

page 21

Fly... 4 left, 3 up, 6 right, 3 up, 1 left, 1 down, 2 left, and 1 up

page 22

page 23

page 24

page 25

page 26

page 27

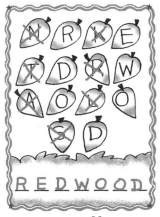

page 28

page 30

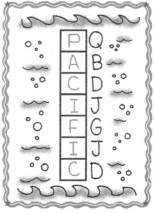

page 31

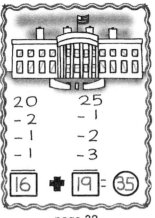

page 32

page 33

page 35

page 37

page 38

page 39

page 40

page 41

page 42